1

Halloween Poems by
The Two Grandmas

Trisha St. Andrews
and
Tera Anne Freese

This is a work of fiction.
Names, characters, places, and incidents either are the product
of the author's imagination or are used fictitiously.
Any resemblance to actual persons, living or dead, events,
or locales is entirely coincidental.

629Publications.com
Trishastandrews.com

Cover Design by Tera Anne Freese and JT Lindroos

Table of Contents

Dedicated to our grandchildren,
Hunter, August, Olive, Tennessee, Lulu,
Rhett, Colt and Sloane,

AND

To all of the children of the world.

REMEMBER:

"Imagination rules the world."

Dear Children,

We hope you love these poems and pictures. We had so much fun creating this book for you and we look forward to sending you more books that make you smile and inspire your imagination.

Hugs from The Two Grandmas.

My Grandmother's Garden

My grandmother's garden has a creepy old gate,
And this year when Halloween comes, I will wait,
Till everyone's sleeping and no one's around,
I'll open that gate and I won't make a sound.

I'm scared of the dark, so I'll carry a lamp,
The moon will be staring, the ground will be damp.
Into the pumpkin patch, I will arrive,
For there all the pumpkins will soon come alive!

Suddenly faces like magic appear,
Some scary like monsters, some funny and queer.
The pumpkins all party and giggle and cheer,
Not knowing that I'm in the garden this year.

When morning arrives, I'll be back in my bed,
While visions of pumpkins all dance in my head.
I won't say a word, because who would believe,
What happens to pumpkins on Halloween Eve!

One Black Cat

All my life I've heard tales about all kinds of cats,
My neighbor's cat Stinky, and one I call Scat!
Some that chase birds, and some that chase rats,
Some that leap, some that sleep, and one acrobat.
Most cats are so charming, incredibly stealthy,
I even met one who's exceedingly wealthy.

But Halloween cats are a whole different breed.
They're scary, too hairy, and not pedigreed.
They eat spiders and bat wings and long centipedes,
And race through your yard at astonishing speeds.
They're sly and they're clever, they're swift and they're sleek,
And if you should see one, you'll freak and you'll shriek.

One Halloween evening, you better believe me,
A black cat approached us with beady eyes gleaming.
His long tail was twitching, his fierce breath was steaming.
I turned to my friends who tried to stop screaming.
We all saw his claws and heard terrible hissing.
The next thing I knew, my friends were all missing.

He stalked as he walked and he glared and he stared.
Suddenly, he said, "Please don't be scared.
It's my job to be frightening. Halloween, you're aware.
I'm just pretending. I know it's unfair.
But just for the record, my name is Dave,
And I think that you are incredibly brave."

Witch's Brew

Spiders, toads, and wings of bats,
Slice of midnight, tails of rats,
Mixed together in a stew,
Come and taste my witch's brew.

Stirring in six pints of blood,
Red as dead, thick as mud,
Sprinkle in some lice, like rice,
Diced up mice. How nice!

Spirits gather, a ghoul, a goon,
'Neath a glaring, staring moon.
Ghosts and goblins fill my room,
While I stir it with my broom.

Floating eyeballs, scrambled brains,
Vampire fangs and entrail stains
Jagged teeth, dragon drool,
Added to my gruesome gruel.

I adore this frightful night.
Witch's brew is my delight.
Chew the chunks of possum feet.
Take a bite of monster meat.

The stew is simmering, almost done,
Boiling, toiling, frightful fun.
Take a sip, if you dare,
It's Witch's brew. BEWARE!!!

Halloween Night

I wonder what I'll see tonight—
Some skeletons or witches?
Or pirates hiding in the trees
Or monsters in the ditches?
On Halloween, my friends dress up
In costumes orange and black.
And if they try to frighten me,
I'll JUMP! and scare them back!

Planning a Halloween Party

"Who shall we ask to our Halloween party?"
Said Blondie the Zombie to Goldie the Ghost.
"Who do we know who is fun and not tardy?"
Said Goldie the Ghost who agreed to be host.
"Spider's a fighter and Witch has an itch.
And Addie the Bat flies only at night.
Patty the Rat gathers food in a ditch,
And remember that she likes to bite.
Skeleton, he cannot eat with no tummy,
And Mummy, he needs to unwind.
And I am a ghost whom no one can see
So, I think we are both in a bind.
A Halloween party seems rather daunting.
Let's stick to staring and scaring and haunting."

Superstitions

I'm not superstitious. I believe in science.
I believe in truths and proofs which have my full reliance.
For example, if you step upon a sidewalk crack,
Do you believe that single act will break your mother's back?
Or walking underneath a ladder? Who should even care?
And spilling salt does not require to throw some in the air.
One superstition makes me laugh. It's from my Auntie Stella.
She says that no one in her house may open an umbrella.
I must admit I have some fears and doubts on Halloween.
You'll notice that this little poem Is not on page thirteen.
This holiday has different rules that once a year apply,
When superstitions become fun. I cannot tell a lie.
Seeing cats, especially black can be a bit disturbing.
A ghostly silhouette against a glaring moon, perturbing.
Once a year, a rabbit's foot is placed inside my pocket;
In case a vampire surfaces, my lucky foot will shock it!
And if on Halloween, you break a mirror, if you could…
Cross your fingers and your toes and LOUDLY KNOCK ON WOOD!

The Necklace

The morning after Halloween, I found a little necklace.
I'm telling you, and only you, because I can't be reckless.
I found it lying in a ditch, the charms on it were tangled,
But when I then examined it, alarmed I was, and jangled.
There were charms of bats and owls and a snaggle tooth.
There are charms of cats with scowls (I'm telling you the truth.)
There was a tiny, tiny clock that had a special power.
It had a chime that rang and cackled every single hour.
A little skull and tiny bones, maybe from a rat?
An eyeball and a vampire fang, a tiny witch's hat.
The more I think about it now, I have a slight confession-
I never should have picked it up and kept as my possession.
What most likely happened was a witch who was exhausted,
That night flew by, high in the sky, and on her way, she lost it.
I think I'll go back to that ditch and leave it where I found it.
I don't want her to find me. I shouldn't be around it.
"Return it to the witch's ditch," says my intuition.
What would you do, if you were me, in this strange position?

The Spider and the Bat

"Come into my parlor," said the spider to the bat.
"My web is soft and silky, and we can have a chat.
I will entertain you with my spinnerets and silk.
I will serve mosquitoes and a vial of chocolate milk."

"Come into my parlor," said the bat to the spider.
"I'm a fruit bat so I'll serve you apple pie and cider.
I'll amuse you with my wings and show you how to fly.
Then I'll hang upside down and hum a lullaby."

"I don't think I'd feel safe if I left my web,"
Said the spider to the bat, "I'll stay home instead."
The bat then said, "I've heard the fate of the famous fly,
Who visited your web, and as the poem says, he died."

So, the spider and the bat agreed they'd not convene,
But live another year to scare the kids on Halloween!

Honestly

The haunted house on Elm Street? Have you ever dared?
Don't tell me to go in there. I'm honestly too scared.
Broken windows, shredded curtains, curls of peeling paint.
Don't tell me to go in there. I honestly would faint.
Every year I hear the tales of those who disappear.
Don't tell me to go in there. I honestly feel fear.
You've heard about the floating ghost and the jumping spook?
Don't tell me to go in there. I honestly would puke.
In the window, have your seen that witch who's evil-eyed?
Don't tell me to go in there. I honestly would hide.
I've heard rumors that we'd see skeletons, a ton.
Don't tell me to go in there. I honestly would run.
But if you really want to, go on my behalf.
Then tell me when it's over. We honestly would laugh.

My Monster in the Closet

I keep my monster in the closet. Where do you keep yours?
My friends have monsters under beds and some of them in drawers.
I keep my monster in the closet so my mom can't find him,
Because I know that if she did, she'd never let me mind him.
He's kind of bossy but he's nice. He hides behind my shoes,
And when I see him after school, he giggles and he coos.
I think he gets so lonely whenever I am gone.
He comes from somewhere far away, it's called Saskatchewan.
The only thing he likes to eat is chunky peanut butter,
And when he gets excited, he always starts to stutter.
His name is Gene, his eyes are green; he's seldomly out-smarted.
If he ever disappears, I'd be broken-hearted.
Let me give you my address- It's 107 Lyman.
And if he's ever, ever lost, will you help me find him?

Not Stopping by the Woods on a Creepy Evening

It's strange how nature celebrates this eerie night contrived,
By those who want occasion to be slightly terrified.
Halloween most surely is a time to stay at home,
But if you walk into the woods, be sure you're not alone.

For in the woods, the howling winds compose a scary air.
You wonder if those mostly ghostly sounds are always there.
The swishing in the brittle branches shattering the peace
Are living beasts and other beasts, supposedly deceased?

Leaves bizarrely brush your face and plummet to the ground
While you attempt to hurry home, so dare not turn around,
For suddenly on Halloween, "your woods" becomes a Haunt,
And getting out, and being safe is all that you may want.

Oogie, The Boogie Man

The only boogie man I've ever seen
Lives on a street in New Orleans.
He isn't scary, that's for sure,
He likes to dance, and be assured,
Oogie is not an amateur.

His girlfriend is Louise E. Ana.
She's from Mobile, Alabama.
When they dance, you best beware,
All the people stop and stare.
And songs and clapping fill the air.

What does he dance, you ask? What would he?
Of course, he dances the boogie-woogie.
I have only one request-
Go to see them, I suggest.
Louise and Oogie, they're the best.

35

Halloween Animals

Slithering snakes on withering leaves.
Screeching owls in reaching trees,
Long-legged spiders in woven webs,
Black cats tread dead flower beds.
Rodents climb a nearby fence,
Bats swoop down from hither and hence,
Howling wolves that growl and roar,
Ravens quoting "Nevermore."
If these aren't enough to scare you.
Older brothers double-dare you,
To go outdoors where it is grim,
Until you beg to come back in.

Sounds That Scare Me

Sometimes, I hear knocking … a sudden bump or thump.
At my door, beneath my floor. It always makes me jump.
Sometimes, I hear scary sounds when I'm all alone.
But on Halloween, the sounds are eerie and unknown.
Especially, sounds that make me cower, sounds that could be harming.
It used to happen more than now. Now they're less alarming.
I'll never know what made those noises; creepy, haunting moans.
It's better I forget those voices; ghostly whispers, groans.
As I grow older, I now know that not all things are real.
My imagination grows, but I don't have to squeal.
But I can if I want to.

The Candy Is Mine!

My mom wants me on Halloween to be a ballerina,
But I'd prefer a scary beast, maybe a hyena.
My brother wants to skip it all, he's turning twelve this year.
He thinks he's tough and old enough to hang out with his peers.
He'll miss the candy, gum, and fun. He'll come up empty-handed.
I know he'll come to me for treats. But let me please be candid.
If trick-or-treating is for kids and we do all the work.
Can't we keep all of the loot and not be called a jerk?

Who Who

My name is LuLu. I live on a street,
Where an owl in a tree just repeats and repeats.
The question's the same, not old or not new.
The question he asks me is "Who? Who?"
I have no idea to whom he alludes,
Or why he obsesses; a curious mood.
He's sure single-minded, he just never tires.
He just says "Who? Who?" That's all he inquires.
He hoots and reboots, never changing his tune,
As he "whos" at me under the big harvest moon.
Why doesn't he ask, why, where, when, how?
I didn't imagine who who is till now.
I've decided that maybe he's talking to me,
And needs a new friend. I'll call him Dupre'.
He likes me and although it may not be true,
Now, I pretend he says "Lu Lu."

Halloween Riddles

I'll tell you all the answers first and you can find the riddle.
You can entertain your friends but I will help a little.
Broom mates are two witches who decide to live together.
The living room is the room that ghosts will enter…never.
A mummy simply doesn't have a single special friend
Because he's wrapped up in himself. And that is not the end.
What do you call a Florida witch, lying on the beach?
That's easy, she's a "Sandwich' and you should hear her screech.
You'll never guess the best dessert that ghosts all love and crave-
It is, of course, "I Scream" ice cream. It is all the rave.
Did you know that ghosts, as well, have a favorite fruit?
It's booberries, of course, what else? There is no dispute.

Bobbing for Bob

On Halloween, my mother takes a shiny, silver pail,
And fills it to the very top with water, without fail.
And drops the apples in it.
Thirteen is the limit.

My friends come over and begin the bobbing competition.
Who can bite the most tonight? A game of guts and mission.
A rule was added. Why?
In case there is a tie.

Then Mom drops two more apples; one of them says "Bob".
We hold our breath and watch, as she gives the nod.
The first to bite the "Bob",
Wins the game. Great Job!!

Two Ghosts Collided

Two ghosts collided in the haunted woods,
And I was there to see.
The fog obscured them for a time,
But then their glow began to shine,
And I chose not to flee.

I listened as their talk had begun,
I rubbed my eyes, not believing,
These woods would be haunted by only one,
And if they fought, maybe none.
One ghost would surely be leaving.

But who would win this spooky duel?
Their apparitions spanning.
Which ghost would be the phantom ghoul?
Which ghost would ultimately rule
The woods where I was standing?

Then they detached in gliding shafts,
Diaphanous, glowing stronger.
One left on a road that had a path
One made a new road, on his behalf-
These woods would be haunted no longer.

Halloween Treats

After trick-or-treating's done,
I'll run home to have some fun,
To count my candy, one by one.

The popcorn balls go in one pile,
The gum and apples stretch a mile,
With candy bars in single file.

I think I'll eat a few, then wait
Until the morning when I wake,
Or else I'll have a tummy ache.

The Man in the Harvest Moon

Have you ever seen a harvest moon, have you watched it rising?
Huge and bright and bloody orange on the far horizon?
The Man in the moon is magnified, easier to see.
His face is glaring, eyes are staring, piercingly at me.
It's almost like he is alive, watching every move.
I'm kind of scared for I don't want The Man to disapprove.
I made The Man in the harvest moon a promise to be good.
Because I am, because I can be, and I always should.
Last night I stared at him real hard. No matter what you think,
I saw him stare right back at me and then I saw him wink.

The Queen of Halloween

Carrie Jo, the scarecrow, is the Queen of Halloween.
Her dress is patched with velveteen, and she is squeaky clean.
Her hair is made of ribbons; a triangle, her nose.
She's friendly and outgoing and she even likes the crows.
When she had her interview to be crowned the queen,
"What was her favorite holiday?" It wasn't Halloween!!
The last day of October? She couldn't tell a lie.
So, she answered honestly, "The fourth day of July!"

The Shrieking Tree

It was a dark and stormy night.
If that's trite, I'm sorry.
It's the best way I can think
Of starting out this story.
The tree outside my bedroom
Was blustery and frightening.
The wind, it roared, the branches raged;
The sky was filled with lightning.
But this was not like other trees,
When storms began to peak.
Inside this tree, from deep within,
I heard a monster shriek.
I pulled my covers from my face,
The shrieking sounded clearer.
Between the thunder, I would peek.
The tree, it looked much nearer.
The sound sent shivers down my spine,
Repeating once again.
The tree appeared to reach for me.
Would it stop and when?
The branches lashed my window pane,
I heard the rainstorm howl.
When all at once I saw the shriek.
It was just an owl.
He saw me too and then he flew
To my window sill.
His eyes were yellow; the little fellow
Gave us both a chill.
I smiled at him, he flew away,
And then I thought much harder.
I should have known a tree can't shriek.
Next time I'll be smarter.

The Witch's Broom

Playing hide and seek one day, I hid inside a closet.
I found a broomstick, pointed hat, and witch's cape, or was it?
Late that night, when it turned dark, and all the family slept,
I dressed warmly, walked downstairs. So quietly I crept.
I'd been thinking all day long about their magic powers.
What if I climbed upon the broom and soared to magic towers?
What if I flew to dragon lands or watched the goblins dance?
Or landed on a mountain top or ended up in France?
I ran outside, all dressed and pumped, ready, but perplexed-
How do you take off on a broom? But guess what happened next!
My black cat Silky jumped aboard, he was the broom's ignition.
Above the trees and in the breeze, flying was his mission.
It was awesome to be high and see the world below,
The stars, the lights, the meteorites displayed a stellar show.
My cat meowed, "The time is now to put your broomstick back."
So, home we flew. I even knew where I'd store my pack.
Tomorrow night would be more fun. I would hardly sleep.
This was my special secret, the one I'd always keep.
Who was the witch inside my house? This thought was really wild-
Perhaps my mother is the witch and I'm a witch's child.
But then another thought I had was even more inviting.
Perhaps the broomstick, hat, and cape were meant for me! Exciting!

Dear Children,

These extra pages are blank for you to draw pictures or write poems from your imagination! Have fun!

If you really love what you've done, please share a copy of what you've written and/or drawn, and who knows, it might show up in one of our next books! (Send it to trishalamusic127@gmail.com.)

Hugs,
The Two Grandmas

65